Journey to Louisville

Book 2 of the Porch Girl Series

Terry D. Bible

ROYSTON
Publishing

BK Royston Publishing
P. O. Box 4321
Jeffersonville, IN 47131
502-802-5385
http://www.bkroystonpublishing.com
bkroystonpublishing@gmail.com

© Copyright – 2018

All Rights Reserved. No part of this book may be reproduced, stored in a retrieval system, or transmitted by any means without the written permission of the author.

Cover Design: Brent Barnett for besquareddesign.com
Cover Image by Permission of the Louisville Transit Authority of the River City – Original Louisville Train Station, Louisville, KY

ISBN-13: 978-1-946111-22-7

Printed in the United States of America

Dedication

It is to my deepest gratitude and dedication to my favorite women in the Quinton Family.

GREAT- GRANDMOTHER
Maggie Patton Cannon

GRANDMOTHER
Hattie Mae Cannon Irvin Carter

MOTHER
Jacqueline Lorene Harding Bradley

Acknowledgements

I never would've had this book published had I not listened to my late mother Mrs. Jacqueline Lorene Harding Bradley.

To my dearest friend, Sandra Anderson Bouggess for giving me encouragement and the boldness to succeed in my endeavors. "Hail Central High!

I'm also truly grateful to my insurance agent, Mr. Louis Coleman for selling me a Toshiba 95 Windows Laptop in 2001.

Giving Praises to God for Rev. Gregory Smith of Hill Street Baptist Church for allowing me to have evening classes with him to learn about my computer in 2002.

Thanks to Mr. Tony Holley for being my "Computer Technician" helping me out in the late hours of the night.

Thanks to the Sally Bingham's Kentucky Foundation for Women's "The HopScotch House" for developing solitude and peace even when I was going through a "storm" in my life.

Ms. Shirley Hurley was so kind and patient with me as I browsed through a lot of books in the library and participated in meditation through faith that I will succeed with "Porch Girls".

Foremost and for all, to give thanks to my Lord and Savior Jesus Christ for giving me such fantastic insight and the women in my life as the "seeds of my life" to achieve my goals.

Terry D. Bible

Table of Contents

Dedication	ii
Acknowledgement	v
Introduction	ix
Characters	xiii
Papa John Arrives	9
The Thriving Thirties	15
The 1937 Flood	19
The New Negroes	23
The Segregated Fifties	27
Tisha Mingo Quinton was born	37
Smoketown	47
Josephine Goes to New York	51
Josephine Left for Cleveland, OH	57
The Fabulous Sixties	61
The Flood in Southwick	75
American Crisis	77

Macho Men- Macho Boys   83

Soul Sistahs   93

Introduction

Well...well...well... We had engaged ourselves from treachery to triumph, from viciousness to victory. Our people have died and went on to glory but my people kept moving.

It is now in the 1920s. As Grandma Susie rides the train with her daughters not knowing what it is until she gets there. Since the Quinton Mansion burned down, Susie was so relieved that she didn't have to be in such disparity between families anymore.

Music became a part of Susie's life especially gospel for Mahalia Jackson was soothing her soul to great heights. As her sister Hilda tagging right behind her, this is only the beginning of another life.

White America was streaming down like a river flowing into chaos and distress and it was nothing they could do about it except move out. Segregation flowed from the north, south, and the east except the west end of Louisville, as our people bought their first homes. Television and the music on the radio were fluent still in White America but we dealt with it.

There were some good white people though. Anne and Carl Braden helped a Black couple in Shively get their home until some whites burned a cross in the yard. Yeah we kept on fighting, and we kept on singing, and we kept on caring and we kept on loving.

Josie started to feel nostalgic about her life. When her daughter Tisha Mingo was born and had another child, her feelings took a left shift to what she was wanted to do. So, she decided to take off. Susie, Hilda, and Mr. Bill and his children boards the train to leave

Tennessee until they arrive to Tennessee, Mr. Bill stays on the train to go farther north. John Quinton stays back to deal with the burnt mansion.

In spite of the civil turmults' throughout the country, the people of color just kept on singing, they kept on praying, they kept on caring, and most of all they kept on loving. As they moved from the south to the north, whitey still brought havoc in the community. As we lost our beloved Pres. Kennedy, we mourned badly.

As Pres. Johnson signed the Civil Rights Bill, the "New Negro" turned into Afro-Americans, African-Americans, and Black Americans. Everything but Who we really are... But we kept moving into our music which soothes the savage beasts or shall I say the poor and lowly.

Black America was moving in Detroit, Philadelphia, and Memphis

CHARACTERS

James Wittington-Hilda's companion and Thelma's Father

Thelma- Hilda's and James' daughter- troublesome, man-crazy

Aunt Margaret- Susie's daughter with protruding mouths and beautiful black, curly hair

Hilda- Susie's sister with a flauntly attitude toward men, takes her "white" lookingness to be with the high society Blacks on Peach Street.

Geneva-Susie daughter-Tisha Mingo's grandmother, brown skinned, beautiful hair, protruding mouths.

Dorothea- "Dot" Aunt Margaret's daughter with a round-head, pretty long hair, and very smart

Betty- Geneva's daughter, light brown hair with hazel brown eyes, another wild one

Mary Catherine- Josie and Betty's long lost sister, chocolate brown skinned, with a protruding mouth, intelligent, small build woman but funny.

Samuel Jackson- Josephine, Mary Catherine, and Betty's father

Louie B- Pool Hall owner and Speakeasy owner on Walnut St.

Snoot Toot- a street drinker on Peach Street formally Walnut Street

Joe Downs- not an attractive guy, friends with Margaret and Geneva

Petey- slow talker on Peach St.

Jimmy- friend of Geneva and Margaret

Uncle Ray- Margaret's husband, owned a funeral home

Bernard Jones- blue collar worker, living in the Smoketown area

Uncle Elton- Josie's Uncle, lives in Cleveland, Ohio

Phyllis- Uncle Elton's companion- beautiful "white woman

Lucy- Albert's sister in Cleveland, Ohio

Shayla & Bernard Jr. — Geneva's 2nd set of children, Josie & Betty's brother and sister

Miss Lynn- Josie's bestest friend in Southwick

Miss Hollie- neighbor to Geneva & Margaret, babysit Josie, Betty, and Dot Russell Jr. High- School that the girls attended

Mr. Coles- Science teacher at Russell Junior

High School

Barbara, Jim Dandy, Helen, Babe Brother - Dot, Josie and Betty's friends from the neighborhood

Bernie- Aunt Betty's son

Melissa- Babe Brother's girlfriend
Calvin- Dot's companion

Babe Brother – Barbara's brother soon to be Tisha Mingo's father

Felicia- Dot's daughter with a personality like a duck

Albert Jackson- Josephine's husband

Wendell Bradley- Albert's cousin

Uncle Jim- Josephine, Betty, and Mary's Uncle

Journey to Louisville

Journey to Louisville

It was 1926. Susie, Hilda, Mr. Bill and their children were boarding the train. The conductor hollers "All aboard!" John follows the train until he couldn't follow it anymore. Susie and the children had tears in her eyes, as Hilda held her sister's hand with care in her eyes. The children kept waving as they were crying. Especially Elton; he wanted to stay with his father. He hated that he had to leave Florida to miss his Uncle Will.

When Susie calmed down, one of the porters asked them for some refreshments. He brought Susie the paper. It had an article in it about A. Phillip Randolph, a black man that was fighting for the rights of porters of the train company. It seemed that the porters weren't getting equal pay and benefits.

He organized the 'Brotherhood of Sleeping Car Porters.' Randolph was a powerful man. Susie was also reading about Josephine Baker, a dynamic entertainer that took her talent to New York where she performed some stage productions. She was a beautiful woman with a cross-eyed face. She would wear her hair in waves slicked down her head. She later went to Paris, France to reside.

As the sisters were reading the paper, the children were excitingly looking out the window. After they ate their dinner, Susie took the children to their boarding area. Hilda shook her head to say, "What in the world is wrong with this country? It sure is a lot going on, I tell you."

Susie replied, "That's what happens when you have been stuck on the porch not knowing what the outside world is doing."

Susie talked to the lady to see if she could get the apartment. It had twenty stairs with a banister that was made out of dark oak. The kitchen was small for one person to be in. It had two bedrooms and a big living room with a huge window facing the street. The apartment didn't have closets, so Susie knew that she had to buy at least two armoires.

Hilda found her a house right down the street. So the sisters got busy moving in their new place. The children were happy that they were finally getting settled in. They painted the dingy walls white all the way down the stairs. The kitchen was painted yellow, for it had a small window facing the back of an alley. The kitchen had a back door. In case of a fire, they could go down the fire escape.

Weeks had gone by. Papa John hadn't come to Louisville yet. Susie was getting upset because she knew about that woman name Patty. Susie went to use a phone to call Florida to see what's going on. No one has seen him. Elsie never got in touch with Susie since she had found Jenny.

Susie took her money and put it in a case in her bedroom, for she couldn't take it in the bank. She didn't trust them.

Susie found a job in a laundromat. Elton went off to college in Ohio, and he never came back. All the responsibilities went to the girls. My grandmother Geneva and her sisters went to an all-black school, because they couldn't go to the white schools. It seemed that 'Jim Crow' was in Louisville too. The Quinton girls learned a lot in school.

They learned about Booker T. Washington, W.E. B. Dubois and Carter G. Woodson. They called him 'the father of black history.' They learned about a black man name, Lewis H. Latimer. He invented a device to manufacture carbon filaments used in electric lamps. They also learned about Garrett A. Morgan, a black inventor that patented the three- position traffic signal.

It had been almost two hundred years since the Africans had arrived in this country. For the dedicated men and women to have contributed their talents with all their heart and soul but still couldn't get the integrity and respect due to them, blacks were still considered as second -class citizens. No matter who did what, the system refused to allow such togetherness to be instilled in this country. As the children were growing to be mature teenagers, John still hadn't come to Louisville. Susie was getting discouraged, as she continued right on living for herself. Hilda had her daughter. Her name was Thelma Quinton. She couldn't have her father's name Wittington, because he was white and he didn't have a clue that he had a daughter. So, Hilda took care of her daughter herself.

Papa John Arrived

It was almost Christmas. As the Quinton family was preparing for the holidays, someone knocked on the door. Margaret went to the door, and it was Papa John getting out of the cab. "Mama! It's Papa!" Susie was in the kitchen cooking a big twenty-five-pound ham with pineapples and cherries on top. The girls ran down the stairs to greet their father. Louise almost knocked Geneva down, for she wanted to be the first one to hug him.

They all walk back upstairs, as Susie kept on cooking. John walks in the kitchen to greet Susie: "Hi Susie." Susie kept on cooking, for she didn't give John any embrace. She hollers out. "Come here yaw."

The girls got quiet not knowing what their mother is going to say. "Go over to your Aunt Hilda's house and tell her come here." The girls went to get their coats, for they were glad at least they would get outside in the cold to play in the snow.

Geneva told her sisters, "I vowed to myself that I'm going to get out of here!" "Me too," replied Aunt Margaret. All of a sudden, Aunt Margaret started laughing. "What's so funny Margaret?" Geneva asked. "I feel sorry for you Louise," Aunt Margaret said. Aunt Louise replied, "Bitch, what makes you think that I'm going to stay here?"

"Yaw had no business going to see those men that got a whole lot of women." Geneva rose from her bed and said, "How do

YOU know? Aunt Louise answered with dignity, "I may be young, but I'm not stupid. I remember Aunt Elsie telling me: Chile, don't be like me without no man, no children; living without nothing." Geneva and Margaret listened to their sister, as if they haven't listened to her before.

The next evening, the sisters went home like good primitive church children with respect.

Susie was a church going woman. A Baptist she was and yes, her daughters had to go all day. When Geneva would be in church looking at those boys, Susie would catch her in the eye to give her a look that could kill a mule.

Margaret would just laugh, as she caught a boy in her eye without her mama knowing it.

When people would say: "Every shut eye ain't sleep," Susie would play like she was sleeping to see if they would ease off the porch. She would rise-up to scare the hell out of them with 'the broom.' See, the broom was the only weapon that the parent could use to get the children in line. Not only the broom but a belt, a switch off the tree or an extension cord. These were the weapons that parents used to get their children in line, as they stayed on their porch filled with disillusion, frustration and the ignorance of not knowing what their future may bring.

Even though the Quinton girls were learning about other Negroes making it in this prejudice world of America, it didn't seem that it was affecting them. Because when their mother got them out of Florida, they wanted to strike out on their own; off the porch of pain and disillusion.

Swinging left and right, her daughters would be devastated that they couldn't get off the porch. I guess the porch didn't do them any good, for Geneva and Margaret had their first child out of wedlock. Aunt Hilda had a man to help her with her daughter. He worked at a funeral home uptown.

Thelma was growing up wild like a runaway child. Hilda was having problems out of her. Louise couldn't do anything with her, for their ages weren't too far apart. Louise didn't have the patience to be with Thelma.

The Thriving Thirties

It was the striving 30's. Herbert Hoover was President. Situations were getting harder and harder. The system was still lynching black men and keeping them in the 'chain gang,' to keep the population low. Back then, families were large and strong; full of vibrant energy and strength. The black families had land that stretched way across the county that they had endured since slavery.

The last confrontation my grandma Geneva had with her mother was when Geneva wanted to go out to meet this man. Geneva couldn't take it anymore. Geneva told Susie that she was pregnant. Susie wasn't happy with that. Geneva told her mother that she won't pour another bucket of water on her anymore. Susie hollered out, "Go on! Get out of here. You'll be back."

It was in the year of 1935 that President Franklin Delano Roosevelt was President. He was a powerful man, even though he was stricken with tuberculosis in his legs. He bounced back with strength and stamina with the help of God.

His wife Eleanor Roosevelt and Mary McCleod Bethune was running this country with the racism that had stirred this country with vengeance through these years in America. Geneva had her first daughter name Betty. Betty had sandy brown hair with hazel eyes. Then she had my mother, Josephine in the year of 1937. My mother was dark brown with big Egyptian eyes and Indian black hair. Aunt Margaret had a daughter named Dorothea. She had a big head and was very light bright and damn near white. The aunties called her:

'Dot'. Dot and Betty were born in September.

The 1937 Flood

There was a flood in Louisville in 1937; the Quinton girls were truly blessed. They were not near the devastation in the city, because they were in the middle of the city. It was hard times for the blacks in the city that had to get their goods from uptown. It became hard for them, so they succumbed to taking care of each other to make it in the metropolitan area.

Papa John was dying. Susie and the children went to see him. William had died in Florida. Elsie and Jenny had perished too. So as far as anyone coming for Papa John's funeral, it was a few and far between. No one came to Papa's funeral from Florida.

Susie had to take her sole earnings to bury him.

Papa John told Susie that he always loved her and the children. Even though he gambled his life away, he did leave Susie some money to bury him. What she had left was for her and the children, which was $500.00. Aunt Louise went into oblivion. That's when Geneva and Margaret knew that Louise wasn't going to make it in this world. Because of her Auntie Elsie, did not have a man to experience what it was like to have a comfort of a man instead of just getting pleasure out of it.

Louie B held a pool hall called the 'Majestic Palace' on the famous Peach Street. The New Negroes were barbers, teachers and entrepreneurs with restaurants, a publishing company and many other businesses that were encountered on Peach Street. In the forties, blacks couldn't go farther than Ninth Street. The New Negroes protested downtown.

Whitney Young, Lyman T. Johnson, Georgia Powers, Roy Wilkins and George Unseld held a sit-in at the Walgreen store on Fourth Street. Negroes weren't getting the proper respect to even eat at the restaurants. There were stores like Byck's, Sears & Roebuck and Penney's. You had to be light, bright and damn near white to get a job downtown, unless you were a cab driver or a maintenance man.

The New Negroes

The 'New Negroes' formed their life on Peach Street and the Beecher Terrace area. 'The Jook Joint', 'The Cotton Club' and even the Breck Building that was located on Ninth and Jefferson, were places that the Negroes hung out. It may seem like they were in 'their place', but they were beginning to be more industrious, more professional and technical in their endeavors.

There were three black sisters that held a funeral parlor by the name of 'Williams,' they helped a black man name Calvin Winstead. Calvin Winstead became a very prominent mortician in the city of Louisville. He helped a lot of blacks in the mainstream of the black society. Grandma

Susie was hearing what was going on Peach Street.

By her working all the time, she didn't have a chance to do anything with her daughters cutting up. It took Aunt Hilda while she stayed in the limelight, to tell about the so-called indignant black folks with clout about their functions. Aunt Hilda was going to a banquet that evening.

The school system had Truant Officers that would come to your house to see why you're not in school. This is where Betty comes in, because she never wanted to go to school. She was always fighting girls as well as the boys. As Dot would go to school without any problem, Aunt Hilda wanted to keep Dot and not Josephine or Betty. Aunt

Hilda treated them like she had done her nieces by making sure they had clean panties on before you sit on her sofa.

Betty cursed Aunt Hilda out and broke her window. Susie was heated. She went to the school to help Betty get back in, after a teacher slapped Betty because she was cutting up. Susie went to the school and the teacher jumped out the window. The class went berserk. The principal had to come and calm them down. The principal even laughed. Susie didn't play.

Geneva and Margaret were terribly concerned about their children. Since they had gotten married, they both worked on second shift which was hard for them to tend to their girls. Susie did everything anyway.

There was this park on Seventeenth and Magazine. It had a pool with quite a lot of swings for children to swing in. Josephine would buy herself some 'funny books' with Archie, Jughead, Veronica and Betty at Riverview High, Dot and Casper the friendly ghost, and she would go to the park to read.

The Segregated Fifties

The 'Segregated Fifties' were getting to be exciting for the girls. Rock and Roll was in. Even though their parents liked jazz and blues, a lot of black artists were coming out singing full force. There was Fats Domino, Dinah Washington and Etta James. And for the white folks, there were Jerry Lee Lewis and Elvis Presley. My mother Josephine, Dot, and Betty had the stylish clothes.

There were five women that changed Louisville in the fifties. Their names were Anne Braden, Hattie Bishop Sneed, Mae Street Kidd, Georgia Powers and Elizabeth Breckinridge. By Miss Kidd passing for white, she became the first black representative that won her seat in Congress. She helped legislate the 15th Amendment that helped blacks get decent housing. Anne Braden, a white woman and other white liberals helped her. Josephine and Dot were excelling in their endeavors at school. Dot became a majorette at Louisville Central High School. Josephine was in the Bugle Corps. As far as Betty was concerned, she disappeared completely out of the school system. She beat up the Truant Officers. They wouldn't go get Susie anymore. She would come around but didn't mention school. She would run like a deer in the woods. She loved the streets.

Betty loved the streets so much that she developed an addictive behavior in drinking. Josephine and Dot would drink

Créme of Soda with gin in it. When Dot got drunk, her speech would be so slow that my mother Josephine would laugh at her on purpose. Things were getting better for the Quinton family. Their mothers would go to the Breck building to attend those dances.

My Aunties and grandmother would be so sharp with their black, pink and green chiffon dresses with the scarves to match. My uncles and grandfather would have on their tuxedoes looking like a million dollars. The girls stayed with Susie that evening. Susie told her granddaughters. "Yaw going to be just like yaw's mama. Can't pour piss out of a boot," she laughs out loud.

Susie asked Josephine: "Where's Betty, black gal?" Josephine answered while eating some maple nut ice cream. Dot would be eating orange sherbet.

"I don't know Big Mama. I went to tell Daddy on her, and he just looked at me all funny." Susie said.

"Um, hum. That's all right. Her ass is going to be just like Thelma. She's going to be always into trouble. Lord, Lord, Lord. I just don't know why or where they getting this devilish shit from."

Dot would give Josephine 'the eye' to see if they can go out. Josephine finished her ice cream. As she walked toward the kitchen, she turns around to ask her grandmother with an innocent look on her face: "Big Mama, can we go to the park? We'll be back before it gets dark."

"Black gal, yaw better be back here, for you don't want me to come looking for you." Susie said smiling with her snuff can beside her chair. She spits in it.

"Thanks Mama," Dot and Josephine snuck out the door.

Happy as a lark! Laughing down the street, Dot and Josephine couldn't wait until they see their friends. Barbara, Jim Dandy, Helen, Babe Brother and Cedric Turner were waiting on them at the park. They're planning to go to the 'Gut Bucket' tonight. Just a little while before it got dark, Josephine and Dot couldn't wait to get their hands on something to drink.

As they turned the corner on Magazine, Babe Brother sees my mother. He smiles and runs up towards her.

Cedric was waiting for Dot. "Where's Barbara, Helen and Jim Dandy?" Dot asked. Babe replied: "He's gone to get us some Falls City beer, some cigarettes and some gin." Dot said, "Ooh wee, we're gonna have some fun tonight."

Babe Brother was a fine teenager. He had coal, black, wavy hair with dark thick eyebrows like actor Tyrone Power.

His mustache was even black and thick. He was not all that tall, but his physique made him look gorgeous.

"Now, yaw want to throw it away? Why can't yaw wait until yaw get out of school at least?" Josephine didn't know, but she was already pregnant. Josephine started crying. "I'm sorry Mama." Susie looked at Josephine as if to already know.

"Oh Lord, my granddaughter has hurt herself." Dot stood there with her head down. Susie looked at Dot. "Oh Lord, don't tell me you too!!! Dot's eyes got big to say. "No ma'am, I'm not pregnant!!!

Susie gets on the phone to call Geneva. Geneva really didn't expect Josephine to get pregnant so early. Betty had already had a boy. While she still goes out in the streets, Betty would leave her son with Josephine because Geneva worked and so did Susie. Josephine went to school in Smoketown until she started showing. The Counselor would come to my grandmother's house on Clay Street to see that my mother Josephine comes back to school.

Geneva calls Babe Brother's family to meet with them. It wasn't a pretty situation. The Thomas family wasn't happy about their son getting a young girl pregnant. Hell, he was young himself. Everybody was arguing about whose too good for each other, not getting married and other issues involving child support.

After the confrontation was over, denial sat in with my father's family. They insisted that my father should not marry my mother. They found out that Babe Brother their son was having an affair with some chick in the projects called 'The Terrace.' They didn't say anything to him then, because she was a light, bright and damn near white chick. My mother was very badly hurt. Josephine stayed with her mother for a while, because Betty kept leaving her son with grandmother Geneva.

Melissa said: "I'm with Babe, because he wants me to be with him. We're going to California as soon as the baby is born." Josephine said angrily: "You bitch! Nothing is going to come out good in yaw's relationship, because you're taking my child's father away." People were out seeing if there's going to be a fight. Babe Brother found out about it. His family found out about it too. They were not pleased at all even though they liked the way the girl looked.

Tisha Mingo Quinton was Born

Josephine didn't say anything to Babe until December 11, 1953. Six months had gone by before Babe came around Josephine. My dad came to the hospital to see us. I was a beautiful baby girl with long, black hair going down my neck. I had his dark eyebrows as well. Babe's sister came to see if the baby girl looked like her brother.

Josephine was really sad but happy at the same time. Josephine's birthday was two weeks away. She couldn't wait to get out and party. Susie came to see us too. She was really happy to see me. I was a beautiful baby that looked like a hairy, little kitten. My grandmother Geneva wanted my mother to name me Tisha Mingo Quinton. My daddy wasn't happy with that. He gave me his name Thomas. Whether that made any difference; it didn't.

When my mother Josephine came home from the Louisville General Hospital, she was glad because that was the only hospital that blacks could go to. The hospital looked like a giant prison with the ugly big pipes hanging from the ceiling. It had an odor that wouldn't quit. Drunks and all kinds of dialects came to that hospital.

We stayed on Clay Street with my grandma Geneva. My grandma placed us upstairs in her house with a pot-bellied stove to keep us warm. Josephine didn't like it for some reason. She always had strong intuition about things. Like as if someone had died up there.

One night as she placed me beside her, the stove started smoking. As it was getting stronger, my mother sweated in the bed and couldn't move. She didn't remember hollering for my grandmother, but as my grandmother was coming up those steps, my mother seen a beautiful angel with long, black hair telling her that everything was all right. My mother was steadily hollering.

My grandmother rescued us from the attic. My mother got herself together and called a cab to go to Grandma Susie's house. My mother wouldn't go on Clay Street for a long time. My daddy worried about us. He fell in love with me. I looked just like him.

Grandma Susie allowed Babe to come to see us.

By the time I was two years old, Dot had graduated from Central in 1955. She went to college for a while. Betty would be doing the same thing. My daddy came over on Clay Street to bring me a pretty strawberry dress. I remember twirling around in that dress. I didn't remember my daddy after that. He left to go to California. He really wanted us to be with him. My mother was very sad.

This was when the drama began. Dot came back from college. She was pregnant with her first child, Felicia. Dot stayed on Jefferson Street upstairs from the funeral home with Aunt Margaret and Uncle Ray.

They would play '<u>I Only Have Eyes for You</u>' by the Flamingos, '<u>Only You</u>' by the Platters, '<u>Save the Last Dance for Me</u>' by the Drifters, '<u>Stand by Me</u>' by Ben E. King and '<u>For Your Precious Love</u>' by Jerry Butler. Over and over again, they would play these songs.

Apparently, they got their heart broken. With my daddy being gone, his family never came and saw about me. Dot had caught herself up the same way. Dot was a pretty light skinned woman that looked like an angel to me.

Betty wouldn't come over and be with them. She couldn't be like ordinary people that had babies and be around other women that relate to the issues of Motherhood. Dot's baby was a girl that looked just liked her. Felicia was a pretty brown skinned baby with no hair. Babies with no hair will wound up with a lot of hair as they get older. My Aunties and grandmother was constantly going to the Breck building looking fabulous in their after five wear.

Great-grandma Susie moved into these projects called 'Cotter Homes.' She lived upstairs, which never failed. She didn't want anyone to break into her house. Josephine would stay with Susie, because all of her friends that she went to school with moved in the projects. The same people that lived in the Russell Area obviously needed better housing.

Dot got married. Josephine was alone again. Aunt Louise came back from

California. She found out about Betty and her gregarious behavior. Aunt Hilda died. Cousin Thelma was all alone. She didn't have anything to do but to start meddling in everybody's affairs in the family.

Josephine loved staying with Susie. Josephine had her friends to relate with. In the fifties, there was this park called 'Chickasaw.' In that time, there were three major black neighborhoods: 'Russell,' 'California,' (that was located off 18th Street) and the 'Parkland area' (located in the west end around 26th and Wilson/ Little Africa) part of which is now the Chickasaw area.

Since the fifties, more African-Americans moved into the Chickasaw area with the migrating of the Whites to the suburbs. Chickasaw also had its own quarterly newspaper talking about middle-class blacks, their business and social affairs. It was called: 'The Louisville Defender.' It was founded by a black man named Alvin Bowman in 1933 until Frank Stanley took over in 1936. Willis Cole in 1917 had a newspaper called 'The Louisville Gazette.'

Lyman T. Johnson was a teacher at Central High School. He taught Albert Jackson there. Everybody in Cotter Home went to Central. For those middle-class black children to go to any other school such as Eastern, Manual, Shawnee, and Male, their I.Q. had to be very high.

Nevertheless; despite of the 'System' trying to keep blacks behind in their education, blacks were excelling beautifully without question. Still, the whites didn't want blacks to come to 'their" schools.' In 1955, the new Central High School was placed on 1130 West Chestnut. The "Class of 1955" became history.

My mother and my grandmother were pregnant at the same time, in the year of 1956. My grandmother had her son Bernard Jr. first, while my mother Josephine had her son the same year in November. Albert's mother wasn't happy with that situation.

Smoketown

Aunt Margaret took up for Josephine to Albert's mother. They got to be closest of friends. Aunt Margaret lived in Cotter Home also. My brother Albert Jr. looked like his father. He stayed with Albert.

My grandmother Geneva still lived on Clay Street (which was called 'Smoketown).' Uncle Elton finally came to Louisville. He was a big man. He fell in love with Bernie and I. He had plenty of money. Great-grandma Susie was so happy to see him that she cried for hours. Everybody was at Susie's house. She cooked chicken and dumplings, cabbage, okra with greens and cornbread.

With the commotion about Josephine and Albert, Uncle Elton asked my mother would she come to stay with him. Josephine was ecstatic. It seemed that Albert liked another woman that his mother liked. Josephine was sad again.

While Dot was pregnant with her third child, Betty was still going out in the streets leaving Bernie with Susie. Thelma and Louise were getting closer being that they were just alike those hard, core Quinton women from Tallahassee.

Josephine talked things over with Geneva to let her go to New York to see her Daddy's brother, Uncle Jim. Uncle Jim was a quiet private man. He was a street man, but he had some dignity to his personality. He was a ladies man even though he had a son by a beautiful woman that wind up in a divorce. Geneva thought it was okay. Josephine packed her things and took the train to New York. She told Uncle Elton that she would come to him after her trip.

It was settled. Josephine caught the 'A Train' to New York. I was three years old. I cried all the time. I never knew why, except the fact that my Daddy wasn't with us. My mama knew why, but she kept her feelings within herself.

Josephine Goes to New York

As we arrived in New York, the buildings to me looked like monsters. I really cried then. Not knowing where I was going, and where my mama was taking me. Susie was my heart. I missed her presence around me, that's why I cried so much. Josephine caught a cab to get to my Uncle Jim's house. The cab driver knew that my mother wasn't from New York.

As he got her to her destination, the only thing he said to her: "Always know where you're going. For they could take you anywhere, and kill you and your child." My mother looked at him so puzzled. Because of her coming from the south, the north was very different. Josephine got out of the cab to holler to my Uncle. "Uncle Jim! Uncle Jim! People start looking out their window to see whom this strange person is hollering for someone. My Uncle Jim came out of his apartment to say, "Josie! Girl, don't be hollering for me! What are you doing coming up here? How come you didn't tell me that you was coming?"

My Uncle Bernard Jr., saw I was older, but still crying to be fed.

Josephine got busy in the kitchen fixing formulas and getting the diapers in place, so it would be easier for Geneva to handle the situation. Geneva knew that she needed her daughter to do things. Betty finally came with Bernie. Oh Lord, it was a miniature nursery on Clay Street.

For the first time in a long time, the Quinton women were relating in deep love for one another. They put us to sleep. Josephine found out that Albert had been playing her. Of course, Betty had to tell her. Josephine was furious. She knew that she was going to leave again. As she told her sister Betty about New York, Betty had wished that she had went to New York.

Betty and Josephine sat outside on their mother's steps. Josephine told Betty that in New York they called their steps the 'Stoop.' Geneva had three steps in front of her house. It had a lot of side yard not in the front, but a gate to come in. You had to get a chair to sit outside which was okay.

Josephine told Betty that Uncle Jim said for her to do right.

Betty said, "I ain't thinking about what Uncle Jim thinks. You know me Josie." As they sat outside as it was getting late. Smoketown was a dangerous community. People would shoot their guns, carry their knives, and would fight you as soon as you bat your eye over anything that concerns what they would be into. There were some projects called 'Shepherds Square.' Shepherd Square was just like Cotter Home, but more ruthless. Men were having babies by other women in the same area. Women would fight in broad daylight to midnight over their men. Betty knew all of them. Betty told Josephine about this joint called the

'Top Hat.' You could have a good time in there, until someone gets the shooting. They stayed up all night conversating about how times are flying, until some people that they knew came to talk to them. They talked about the time when they went to Florida, to have a good time with their country cousins. My mother ran into slop of cow manure because one of her cousins ran behind her with a snake in his hand. Josephine had to take a bath in a big tin tub.

    To keep her mind off Albert, Josephine laughed until her stomach hurt. One of the babies started crying. The people left, because they were making too much noise. Geneva was resting quietly, for her son was wearing her out.

Betty stayed with grandma Geneva to help her out. Josephine was glad of that, because Josephine left again to Cleveland to see Uncle Elton.

Josephine Left for Cleveland, OH

My Uncle Elton was glad that my mother arrived to Cleveland. He had a nice, light-skinned lady that had long black wavy hair. Her name was Phyllis Tyler. She came from Texas. She took us in and fell in love with me. I was four years old. My mother taught me how to read. I was a smart little girl with long wavy thick hair, and my eyebrows stood strong on my face like my Daddy's.

There was a lot of talk about President Harry S. Truman signing a legislative bill to segregate blacks in the military. Ever since the Boston Massacre, the French and Indian War, the War of 1812, the Civil War and World Wars I and II, blacks has participated in Freedom for this country of America. Yet in the 1950's, whites still wouldn't accept them in any endeavors that they achieved in. My Uncle was a strong advocate for civil rights. Being half white, it didn't make any difference to him what happened in Florida when he was a little boy. Even though he was named after his grandfather, Uncle Elton told Josephine that he couldn't stand him. Uncle Elton didn't care for his Aunt Hilda, because he said that she was 'color-struck.' "My poor baby sister," Uncle Elton said pitifully. "She's just like them white people."

After she saw that her daughters married these men, she saw that they were more productive than a light-skinned black man. Consequently; she didn't care if they produced and provided for family by giving her money. She was all right with that.

Albert bought me a purple tricycle and some cowgirl boots. I was happy. I start liking him. I start having this feeling of euphoria about him. He was nice to my mother, and my brother and sister were happy too. Dot moved next door with my mother in Southwick. Aunt Margaret moved out of Cotter Homes to live in a house not far from her kin. Aunt Margaret would laugh at her sister Geneva, as she would be in agony with her in-laws.

The Fabulous Sixties

I was seven years old. In the sixties, music changed people all over the world. Chubby Checker, a black music artist came out with a dance called <u>The Twist.</u> The Motown sound came along, and Josephine picked up her spirits to buy the music of: 'Otis Redding,' 'Chuck Jackson,' 'Carla Thomas' and 'Aretha Franklin.' Along with: 'The Temptations,' 'The Supremes' and 'Smokey Robinson.' Louie Beaumont, the man that my grandmother Geneva used to see, died. My mother went out of it. The 'Majestic Palace' turned out to be no more, because no one couldn't take care of it. In fact, Peach Street was going down. The black businesses were moving to other locations in the city. Louie Beaumont had a big funeral. I remember when I was three years old. Mr. Louie would give me money and smiled at me, because I looked like my mother in which he loved dearly.

The drunks, the homeless men and of course a lot of women was going to miss him dearly. Louie would be like a 'social worker' to blacks. He would talk the men into going home to their wives. He would talk the young men coming up in life into going to school. He wouldn't let young boys hang around his joint. He left my mother all his jazz albums from the forties. Louie had Red Foxx, Pigmeat Markham and Moms Mabley albums. My mother played Duke Ellington's: <u>'Take the A Train,'</u> and cried her eyes out.

As quiet as it was kept, Geneva cried silently even though she was married. My grandfather Milt and Jimmy was there and they were all so sad. There was talk about a black man name James Meredith in Mississippi. He attended University of Mississippi. It took the National Guard to guard him the four years that he stayed there until he graduated. While there was a lot of fighting going on in the south, Louisville was missing a good man name Lewis B. Beaumont who was in the Louisville Defender. The Louisville Defender was a newspaper for blacks that told what was going on in the city.

We moved in another building in Southwick where my mother had my little brother. We needed more room for our growing family. Dot moved also, but we could see her back door as she could see our front door. Dot had another baby boy. Then it was eight of us. Of course, Grandma Geneva had a beautiful baby girl. She looked like her husband's people. She had light-bright skin with long beautiful hair and those big eyes with long eyelashes.

In Southwick, everybody took care of each other. They borrowed toilet tissue to a cigarette at twelve o'clock in the morning. People were borrowing at all hours of the night. My step-father Albert, was one of the maintenance men working for the city. He wouldn't allow teenage boys in to get the trees. My stepfather was like a lion in the jungle when it comes to social relations in the projects.

In the 60's, music was changing all around the world. There was this group called: 'The Beatles.' They were sweeping the nation with a song called '<u>We Can Work It Out.</u>' The Beatles soothe the prejudice and pain, when they sung that song. Then you had 'The Beach Boys' with '<u>Good Vibrations.</u>' Their music had that California atmosphere. Elvis Presley was making movies with Ann Margaret. Ed Sullivan had the best show on television. As it came on Sunday nights, blacks would watch: 'The Supremes,' 'The Temptations,' 'Smokey Robinson and the Miracles,' 'The Shirelles' and 'Patty Labelle and the Bluebells.'

There were groups that were name after animals: 'The Animals,' 'The Monkees,' 'Three Dog Night,' 'The Turtles' and 'The Byrds.' There were other outstanding groups called: 'The Doors,' 'Steppin Wolf,' 'The Four Seasons,' 'GrassRoots,' 'The Rolling Stones with Mick Jagger,' 'Blood, Sweat & Tears,' 'The Righteous Brothers' and 'The Chamber Brothers.' There were three radio stations that we listened to. They were 'WKLO,' Cliff Butler had 'WLOU' with gospel music. 'WAKY' and 'WLOU.' The white man still had everything in control. 'WKLO and WAKY' stayed on all night, while 'WLOU' had to go off at six o'clock in the evening. Tobe Howard, a black man that was light-bright damn near white had it going on 'WLOU.' He would have this black couple name Ruby Dee and Ossie Davis tell stories about black cultural life.

They would have this commercial name: 'By The Way' by Joe Black. Joe Black would tell what black men and women had contributed in America.

From inventions to entertainment life, blacks were learning something on the radio. When 'WLOU' would go off in the early evening, my mother Josephine would play her Victrola with some: 'Bill Withers,' 'Lou Rawls,' 'Chuck Jackson' and 'The Isley Brothers.' Smoketown was getting worse. I liked to go see my Grandmother Geneva. I met some friends. My grandmother had some friends that had three sons. They would chase me around those long blocks not once, but three times a day. I came to like two of them. Raymont and Wilson were some handsome boys. One day my grandmother allowed us to go to Shelby Park to swim. I was ecstatic.

As I put on my swimsuit, I didn't realize that you don't leave your underwear on. As the boys tried to teach me how to swim, my underwear showed up like I had balloons on to keep me floating in the water. I was so embarrassed. They stopped teaching how to swim and laughed at me all day.

When night fell in Smoketown, the children had to stay in their yards because of shooting at night. There was a joint down the street where women danced on the bar.

Limousines would be parked all the way to the next block. My Grandmother had a floor model color television. This show that we would watch was called" 'The American Heritage.' It showed films about blacks named: 'Harriet Tubman' and 'Frederick Douglas.'

It didn't stay on long, because the 'system' didn't want us knowing about our people from long ago. The System was stirring up controversy about blacks, because it exploited us as being slaves. I was upset, because I wanted to know. My friends would laugh at my thoughts and ideas about 'black life.'

So, children my age and younger had to deal with: 'Walt Disney,' 'Ed Sullivan' and white musicals with stars like: 'Fred Astaire,' 'Shirley Temple,' 'Ginger Rogers,' 'Gene Kelly,' the black brothers name 'The Williams Brothers' and 'Bill Robinson.' They would dance to their highest horizons of life. The next morning, Stephen had a talk with my parents about how I felt about him staying at the house.

My mother came to talk to me, "Tisha, Uncle Stephen is a good man. He's not going to hurt you. If you think that you're in danger, you could go back to stay with Grandma Susie." As I held my head down to the floor not knowing what to say, I felt this queasy feeling in my stomach. I said, "Okay, I'll accept Uncle Stephen. Even though, I know he's not your brother Mama. I know better."

She laughed at me, and hugged me with her love. I went to stay with Great-grandma Susie. Talking about music to my great-grandma's ears, she would moan like an Indian. That wailing sound as if she was chanting or something like that. As she listens to Mahalia Jackson sing, 'Precious Lord' and 'Go Tell It On The Mountain,' Susie would be crying with joy.

I thought something was wrong with her. At the age of eight, I called Grandma Geneva, Mama and Aunt Margaret to come to see about 'Big Mama.'

When they arrived at her house, Susie was cooking some chicken and dumplings.

Susie looked surprised to see her family, "What's wrong with yaw?"

"Tisha called us to tell us that something was wrong with you Mama," Mama said as her mother and Aunt looked concerned. Susie burst out laughing, "I was listening to Mahalia Jackson on my Victrola." Her stomach was rolling like Santa Claus on Christmas Day. Everybody started laughing too. They knew that I was different from the other children. I took everything seriously.

At the 'Wick,' spring came so gracefully. The cool breeze was swaying to and fro. Susie had these beautiful tall flowers in her small yard in Cotter Home. She dared anyone to pick off of them. There was a wood factory not too far from us. The older teenage boys would go and steal wood, so they could make scooters.

The boys would take the wheels off of old skates to make them roll. Some of the boys would put bottle tops on them to dress them up. I had Bernie to make me one. Since I played with boys more than the girls, I wanted to have everything that the boys had including marbles to bow and arrows. My grandmother would make me play with my dolls for some reason, I didn't know why?

My grandmother Geneva had a sister-in-law name Aunt Clara at the Presbyterian Center in Smoketown. Aunt Clara's son went into the Marines to be in the Vietnam War. Aunt Clara was a teacher. She was so smart that she would drink all the time trying to teach my Uncle Bernard to be smart, but he wouldn't go for it. He was too bad to be smart. He would sell my grandmother's old Jet magazines on the street for fifty cents. The neighbors would come and tell my grandmother. She would whip Bernard Jr. But no matter how much she would whip him, he would find something else to get into.

The Flood – Southwick

It was in the month of April 1963. It rained and thunderstorm for hours. It rained so hard that the Ohio River rose fast upon the dry land in the Chickasaw Park. It had rained so hard that the water had gotten far and beyond its regions to Southwick. It flooded Southwestern Parkway all the way to 39th Street. The news was on TV heavily, as people had to evacuate from their homes.

We were scared because the water was coming to our street. Everybody started packing up to leave the 'Wick.' Grandma Geneva was happy and laughing at the same time. Smoketown was cracking on us. They said that we were beginning to be 'river rats.'

Smoketown had a lot of joints to go into. My parents knew a lot of people. Some of Albert's cousins lived in Shepherd Square, as they partied all day long. It was November 1963; President Kennedy was going to Texas with his beautiful wife Jackie. November was cold that year. As we were looking at television, President Kennedy had arrived in Texas to be in a parade. My brother's birthday was in two days. Mama was preparing for his birthday party. Albert Jr. was excited. I was too. Uncle Bernard and Aunt Shayla came down to stay with us.

American Crisis

As we were looking at television, a terrible thing happened right in front of our eyes. President Kennedy got shot in the head twice. As his body went down in his wife's lap, Governor Connolly from Texas got shot too. The phone got to ringing off the hook. Mama started crying, screaming and hollering. Miss Lynn ran over to our house, for her and mama to hold each other while they share the pain that we as black folks are going to face.

For days, that's all that was on television. Everybody in the nation was crying. They showed a black man playing a bugle as tears rolled down his cheeks. The media showed his little boy saluting his daddy. When we saw that, we cried even more. What happened next was Jackie Kennedy was put on a plane to see that Lyndon Baines Johnson be sworn in as President.

It was told that she didn't want to be there when that happened. America was distraught. While the Vietnam War was still going on, the riots throughout the cities in the nation was rising. America had to go through a terrible, tragedy in losing one of the best Presidents the country had ever had. Martin Luther King was a fighter for peace.

Malcolm X even felt bad saying something like: 'a chicken going to his roost.'

"Where's Albert, Tisha? Tisha, its' going to be war all over America," Mama continued to say. "Look at what's happened since President Kennedy died. People are saying that President Johnson had something to do with it."

I think that white man named J. Edgar Hoover from the FBI had something to do with it. He's watching the Black Panthers, and don't you know that he's trying to get Elvis Presley to 'watch' them? J. Edgar Hoover went through eight presidents and no one is stopping him."

Tisha was astonished. As her face turn with so much fright, Tisha continued to look at the news. By the time Albert came into the house, he had heard the news already. He slumped down in the chair to start crying. "What's going to happen next? Josie. Let's hurry up and get out of here."

The next day, Albert and Mama went to look for a house. It was in the Chickasaw area. Since the whites moved out, the blacks had moved in for about ten years. Mama came back to tell me that she didn't like the house. Anyhow, they bought it anyway.

Albert and Mama argued about the situation which made matters worse, because we wanted to get out of the 'wick' fast. Politically speaking, the 'system' continued to keep the black man down while the black woman rose to a lot of occupations that kept the black man from getting them. Divorces were rising in the black population.

More women were becoming the head-of-the household, as the black man was getting pushed to the side of <u>inadequacy.</u> As the Temptations sang: "it's a 'Ball of Confusion.'"

No one really realized that when President Kennedy stopped Fidel Castro from blowing up America, we could've been gone. Nevertheless, the blacks were still being put aside. I guess we'll never know what President Kennedy might have done, had he lived.

Macho Men- Macho Boys

Isn't it funny how the black man have come a long way- from slavery, to nigga, to the "New Negro" and to be young, gifted, and black? Back in the time about three hundred years ago, America had **real** men. I mean men that would kill for their family.

They provided their wives from buffalo skins to today's polyester. They would work from sun up to sun down. They would rest on the weekend and pray to GOD every Sunday. They would bust their asses for the "massa" to come home to be waited upon like a Japanese warrior.

I couldn't understand the concept from nakedness to zezabelts, from zezabelts to polyester, from polyester to Botany 500. Men of today have forgotten where they came from. They have become to be the "New Negro".

Regardless of the times changing, the man took care of **his** woman. They would open the door for you. They would buy you diamond rings without question. They would wine and dine you until the sun comes up and now they call it "going Dutch."

From our famous brothers from the 1800's to the 20th century, black men were strong, that wasn't afraid to struggle for **change**. My Grandfathers and Uncles had businesses that succeeded well in their endeavors. They kept my Grandmother and Aunties in line.

Now the men has become to be a natural man, a soul man, a blue-collar man, a pimp, and don't forget the homosexual man. How could this big change come upon the black society that has stirred them away from their goals of destiny? **CHANGE**.

Since the sixties, society was throwing a new ball game by allowing women to have men's jobs such as engineering, real estate, and in blue-collar factories. More men were leaving their homes, so they could find jobs while the women were going to college attaining degrees in law, medicine, and other professional jobs.

While the men "slept", the women "creeped" into politics, education, and many other technical employment. Men were teaching their sons how to be a "player". It was a fight going on around the world. Women were uniting against the "slavery" of their men keeping them in "their place" having babies and staying home.

In the seventies, blacks were hitting the movies big. There movies with Geoffrey Cambridge, Moses Gunn, Thalamus Mesulah, *"Come Back Charleston Blue,"* Richard Roundtree in *"Shaft."* Bill Cosby and Sidney Poitier in *"Uptown Saturday Night,"* Calvin Lockhart in *"Cotton Comes to Harlem,"* '*The Mack,"* *"Superfly"* and James Earl Jones in *"The Great White Hope."* There were other movies like *"Mandingo"* and *"Drum."*

There were other actors like Ivan Dixon and Yaphet Kotto that played in a movie called "*Nothing But A Man.*" The movie depicted black men as second-class citizens in White America.

These movies develop the "black power" into the black men to be or not to be in their society. The pro and con of these factious roles turned a lot of black men to lose themselves into an oblivion of inadequacy, inconsistency, and above all to lose their will in the power of God.

While the black man was getting "nigga rich" in his endeavors, the black woman would hem him up with debt in the household. Divorces rose high and the baby still needed a pair of shoes. The black men spirit was "swinging really low" from chains of slavery until the "fighting" seventies.

Change killed the macho men-macho boys in the 1970's. Even though, the changes went in to the next generation. The women helped the cause also. Gone was the respect for one another, gone was the integrity that they had held for years, and gone was the family structure that the next decade had to face.

Since the 1700's, black men were faced with a lot of sexual delimenas, Caucasian women were noticing the black men physiqueness, the white men weren't physically and sexually able to satisfy their women because they were interested in the power of economics to keep America in the bondage of eco- slavery.

Through the 1800's of knowing that Frederick Douglass had a white woman changed the century that proved that a black man could have a white woman to help his status to gain power and prestige in society. Needless to say that the white man burned his newspaper company to shreds, Frederick Douglass moved on.

Black men of the seventies moved on also. In spite of the black families breaking down with the one-parent structure, Black men fought for their rights to keep the struggle going. Black men had their belts of truth on. Black men had their dignity to keep from going to prison.

Everybody was talking about the "country" men from the "city" men and how a difference that it made for the women to strive with them. Really and truly, it was the "country" men that were **real**. They knew how to raise their boys to be men. It was the social-consciousness of the "city" men that permeated the "macho" attitude that men allowed themselves to fall in the foolishness of the movies that falsely portrayed the black men to be or not to be.

To look at Crispus Attucks, Cinque, (pronounced Cin-kay) Dominique Vessey, Nat Turner, Frederick Douglass, Gen. Benjamin Davis, Langston Hughes, James Baldwin, Adam Clayton Powell, Booker T. Washington, George Washington Carver, Thurgood Marshall, Paul Lawrence Dunbar, A. Phillip Randolph, Charles Drew, Dr. Daniel Hale

Williams, Ralph Bunche. ---- These men weren't **macho men** they were **real men** for the cause!

Soul Sistahs

To look back into time, we had some serious "soul sistahs". Josephine Baker, Mary McCleod Bethune, Bessie Smith, Bessie Coleman, Harriet Tubman, Sojourney Truth, Madam C.J. Walker, Shirley Chisholm, Phyllis Wheatley, Barbara Jordan, Rosa Parks, and Angela Davis proved to America that women could do it **alone.**

They gained the respect in society that they didn't have to get married to acquire equal status to man. Some people have all the luck. Some had to set back while others got to the top.

Since Sacajawea, women had reached the "promise land" to prosperity to the ideal building stone in White America today. Our

African sistahs wore their Afros, their corn rolls, with pride. We gained power to conquer our fears as well as our hopes and dreams.

Patricia Harris was the Director of HUD in Washington D.C; while Barbara Jordan was powerful in Texas. Angela Davis was speaking on the unlawful justice involving the "Soledad Brothers." Angela turned my life around as she came to Louisville to speak. Angela had a PHD in Sociology. With her gigantic Afro, she inspired me to the point of no return.

While our Afros were supposed to "represent", J. Edgar Hoover were demolishing the Black Panthers. Our Dashikis went to shreds of pain, to wearing the respect of double-breasted suits and ties. Our Afros went to perms to cutting the hair real short.

All of a sudden, everything went **quiet.** John F. Kennedy, Bobby Kennedy, Malcolm X, and Martin Luther King got assassinated and I think the country died with them.

At one time, the women had care for their children, now its daycare or "the latch-key" children. Our neighborhoods looked terrible and the "system" wasn't allowing our brothers to have a say in their political "seats". Grandma was gone and Papa became a "rolling stone".

Statistics showed that more than 70% women are head of the household today. What happen? The "system" allowed everyone to be on "welfare". From generation to generation, everybody started "sleeping" on the cause of justice.

The mafia, the breakdown of the F.B.I and the C.I.A, National Security and many other organizations poison this nation with **Racism.**

Now that women had struggled to make it better for themselves and their children, men from every race on this earth still fought that this is **their** world. But if they listen to GOD's word in Genesis, the scripture will tell you that women were to be a helpmate **not** a stalemate to man.

Being that different cultures were breaking down through the accommodation of each other to survive, people adapted to what another culture had instead of hanging on to what they had from the beginning. Have you heard that song by Joe Tex <u>"Hold On To What You Got"</u>?

The "system" took our tools of survival, our resources to cultivate to gain our strength to survive. During slavery, the slave woman will have a "doo rag" on her head.

She was being humiliated to represent who she was and where she came from. It was a shame for white women to see our braids to modify themselves to look beautiful.

White men called us "girls", not recognizing us that we were vibrant, lovely women. That's why they "raped" us from our integrity, our strength, and hope. Yet we developed power, triumph, and victory to sustain ourselves to our own identity.

From good, wavy Indian hair, to nappy hair, from brown to red, from straight hair to braids, Black women had identified themselves whatever she succumbed to be. She will be! Amazing for 300 years, this country called "White" America still drilled the semi-consciousness of slavery in our times today. It is called "eco-slavery. The economics of jobs, to credit, and to buying stock and bonds. So instead of jobs, we got prisons, instead of education we got crack on the streets, and if you don't make it- you're DEAD.

To our soul sistahs in the seventies that played in the movies such as Paula Kelly, Rosalind Cash, Alfre Woodard, Diahann Carroll, Ruby Dee, Pam Grier, Lena Horne,

Gloria Foster, Lola Falana, Esther Rolle, Abbey Lincoln, Teresa Graves, Beah Richards, and Ja'Net Dubois made a way out of no way to give love, peace, and understanding in America that black women were capable just like the white women in movies, technology, and many other endeavors in this country.

Nikki Giovanni, Maya Angelou, even Phyllis Wheatley showed the world to put words into peace, harmony, struggle, and love to keep the sistahs in America to keep on fighting for the struggle in our lives to survive!

Althea Gibson, and Wilma Rudolph performed gracefully in Tennis and Track winning the Wimbledon Tournament and the Olympic Gold being gifted, lifted, and blessed!

Mothers, Aunties, Grandmothers, friends of the family had tried to keep their men from going to prison, while they struggled to work for the white man in their homes to put food on the table. The "system" was modeled to allow the black woman to be ahead of the black man. No matter what, the black woman will always be the "head" of the household. To try to demolish a culture of people, the "system" has allowed other countries to laugh at us in peace and war. Now Hispanics are rising and NOW it's their turn!!!

www.ingramcontent.com/pod-product-compliance
Lightning Source LLC
Chambersburg PA
CBHW071140090426
42736CB00012B/2180